P9-DBI-171

Machine
Quilting
with
Alex Anderson

7 Exercises, Projects & Full-Size Quilting Patterns

C&T PUBLISHING

Text © 2007 Alex Anderson

Artwork © 2007 C&T Publishing, Inc.

Publisher: Amy Marson

Editorial Director: Gailen Runge

Acquisitions Editor: Jan Grigsby

Editor: Liz Aneloski

Technical Editors: Teresa Stroin and Franki Kohler

Copyeditor/Proofreader: Wordfirm Inc.

Design Director/Cover & Book Designer: Christina D. Jarumay

Illustrator: Tim Manibusan

Production Coordinator: Kirstie L. Pettersen

Photography: Luke Mulks, unless otherwise noted

Published by C&T Publishing, Inc., P.O. Box 1456, Lafayette, CA 94549

Back cover: *All Geese a' Flying* and *'Round the Twist* by Alex Anderson

All rights reserved. No part of this work covered by the copyright hereon may be used in any form or reproduced by any means—graphic, electronic, or mechanical, including photocopying, recording, taping, or information storage and retrieval systems—without the written permission of the publisher. The copyrights on individual artworks are retained by the artists as noted in *Machine Quilting with Alex Anderson*.

These designs may be used to make items only for personal use or donations to non-profit groups for sale. Each piece of finished merchandise for sale must carry a conspicuous label with the following information: Designs ©2007 Alex Anderson from the book *Machine Quilting with Alex Anderson* from C&T Publishing.

Attention Copy Shops: Please note the following exception—publisher and author give permission to photocopy the pullout for personal use only.

Attention Teachers: C&T Publishing, Inc., encourages you to use this book as a text for teaching. Contact us at 800-284-1114 or www.ctpub.com for more information about the C&T Teachers Program.

We take great care to ensure that the information included in our books is accurate and presented in good faith, but no warranty is provided nor results guaranteed. Having no control over the choices of materials or procedures used, neither the author nor C&T Publishing, Inc., shall have any liability to any person or entity with respect to any loss or damage caused directly or indirectly by the information contained in this book. For your convenience, we post an up-to-date listing of corrections on our website (www.ctpub.com). If a correction is not already noted, please contact our customer service department at ctinfo@ctpub.com or at P.O. Box 1456, Lafayette, CA 94549.

Trademark (™) and registered trademark (®) names are used throughout this book. Rather than use the symbols with every occurrence of a trademark or registered trademark name, we are using the names only in the editorial fashion and to the benefit of the owner, with no intention of infringement.

Library of Congress Cataloging-in-Publication Data

Anderson, Alex,

Machine quilting with Alex Anderson : 7 exercises, projects & full-size quilting patterns.

p. cm.

ISBN-13: 978-1-57120-376-2 (paper trade : alk. paper)

ISBN-10: 1-57120-376-1 (paper trade : alk. paper)

1. Patchwork--Patterns. 2. Machine quilting--Patterns. I. Title.

TT835.A493674 2007

746.46'041--dc22

2006018829

Printed in China

10 9 8 7 6 5 4 3

DEDICATION

Thank you to my friends at C&T Publishing who campaigned for this book. Without your encouragement, I would never have discovered the magic and joy of machine quilting.

ACKNOWLEDGMENTS

THANK YOU TO:

Benartex, Moda, P&B Textiles, Free Spirit, and Robert Kaufman, who so graciously provided wonderful fabric to play with.

Olfa Products, for great tools to work with.

Bernina, for letting me create and play with their terrific sewing machines.

Bob and Heather Purcell of Superior Threads, for their excellent product and for their dedication to educating the consumer about the wonderful world of thread.

The Cotton Patch, for their great products and continued support.

Darra Williamson, for her ongoing support.

Pam Vieira McGinnis, for her talented piecing skills.

Erica von Holtz, for her eagle eye.

Matthew Eich, my talented webmaster, who created the delightful dancing alligator illustration on page 12. It has been a pleasure watching you grow into such a fine young man.

And, of course, the wonderful women who guided my machine quilting journey:

Margaret Gair, who taught me that success in machine quilting is all in the basting.

Paula Reid, who taught me that the size of the quilt doesn't matter; I could quilt a quilt of any size on my sewing machine.

Gloria Smith, who helped it all click by comparing machine quilting to drawing with a needle.

Diane Gaudynski, who taught me that any motif I could quilt by hand I could duplicate on the sewing machine.

Sue Nickels, who reminded me that it wouldn't happen overnight, but that with "practice, practice, practice," I could become a fine machine quilter.

Thank you, one and all!

Contents

Introduction

Welcome to the wonderful world of machine quilting! You are about to begin an exciting journey that will add a whole new dimension to your quilting life.

I have to be honest. When my publisher, C&T, first approached me to write a book about machine quilting, my first thought was "Not me!" Although I had learned to machine quilt about fifteen years earlier, I still found it a bit of a challenge…to say the least! Then, about three years ago, I woke up in the middle of the night and decided I was being foolish. I got up from the bed and promptly held a serious meeting with me, myself, and I. I realized that my lack of confidence in machine quilting was all in my head. I could do it!

That change in attitude made all the difference in the world. I began to approach machine quilting with the same enthusiasm and confidence that I brought to every other area of quilting. Then one day, as I sat at my machine, I realized that my shoulders were no longer attached to my ears. I was machine quilting…and liking it!

I was so excited that when the subject of a book about machine quilting came up again, I was ready to take on the challenge. I wanted to create a book that would give quilters the basic skills they needed to take the plunge, along with exercises and quilts to practice their new skills on. But also—and perhaps more importantly—I wanted to offer encouragement. If I can machine quilt, so can you!

So if you're new to machine quilting, or if you've tried it before but were less than thrilled with the experience, this book is for you.

Consider it a place to start. You'll find basic information about equipment and setup—both physical and mental!— all geared to a novice machine quilter. You'll learn the ABCs of marking and basting, and strategies for planning a quilting path and handling "the bulk." Tips for making clean stops and starts, and for simple but successful straight-line and free-motion quilting come next, all designed with a new machine quilter in mind. Finally, I've kept the projects in this book to a manageable size so your first machine-quilting experience will be a successful one. Most of the projects can easily be enlarged if you so desire.

Once you've got these basics under your belt, I encourage you to take classes from whomever you can. Every teacher has his or her own techniques, and you'll learn something new from every one of them.

Is my machine quilting perfect? No…but it gets better with every quilt I quilt, and I have confidence that this improvement will continue, just as I have confidence that with a good grasp of the basics and the patience to practice, you'll be machine quilting—and enjoying it— very soon.

Happy quilting!

The Equipment

Sewing Machine

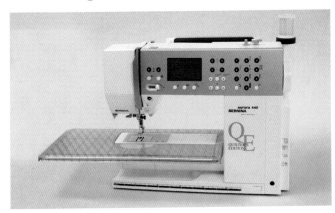

When sewing machines were introduced in the mid-nineteenth century, they were not designed for the way we use them today. No one dreamed of the potential that future machines would have or the demands that future stitchers would put on their machines. The stress on your machine when you are machine quilting is much more than when you are piecing. The stress is constant, and you want a machine that can handle it.

A sturdy, well-maintained sewing machine is your best friend for machine quilting. You want a machine that you're comfortable and familiar with, and one that can handle the demands you will place on it. In short—you want a machine that allows *you* to set the mood of the day, not one that dictates it for you.

Perhaps you already have a sewing machine suitable for machine quilting. Perhaps you are in the market for a new one.

If you are purchasing a new machine, do a bit of research. Visit the websites of the various sewing machine manufacturers. Sewing machine companies love quilters and are eager to introduce new technologies that help make our stitching easier and that have the potential to cut the learning curve dramatically. For example, Bernina has introduced a groundbreaking feature called the Bernina Stitch Regulator (BSR). This innovation sees the fabric as you move it under the needle and automatically regulates the length of your stitches, keeping the stitches consistent in size and making free-motion quilting a breeze.

However, no matter how fine your machine is, it will not perform its best if you neglect to maintain it. If you machine quilt, you are putting *lots* of wear on your machine. Clean and oil it regularly as the manufacturer directs—usually after every six to eight hours of stitching. Be sure to take it in every six to twelve months for professional service. Consider this preventive maintenance; mark it on your calendar, so you don't forget!

tip Carefully consider the reputation of and your comfort with the sewing machine dealer as you decide where to purchase your machine. You are making a big investment and establishing a long-term relationship with someone who can provide valuable education and important service. I think of it as joining a family.

I love my sewing machine—it's a Bernina—for many reasons. Here are some of the key features I look for:

- Needle up/needle down function. This feature does exactly what it says: it allows you to stop stitching with the needle either raised or buried in the quilt. The latter position is especially useful for machine quilting; it enables you to hold your place when you stop to shift or pivot the quilt sandwich. You control this function either by hitting the base of the foot pedal or by pressing a button on the machine.

- Free-hand system or knee lift. This feature allows you to raise or lower the presser foot without removing your hands from the quilt, giving you an extra hand for controlling the quilt.

- Feed dogs that can be lowered or dropped for free-motion quilting (more about this on page 24).

| Feed dogs raised | Feed dogs lowered |

- Good, consistent tension that is easy to adjust.

- A walking foot attachment for straight-line machine quilting. (I prefer an open toe, so I can see where I'm going.)

- Adaptability for an open- or closed-toe darning foot for free-motion stitching.

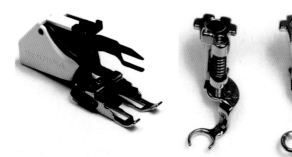

Walking foot   Open- and closed-toe darning feet

Finally, keep in mind that machines have a limited life span and they do—eventually—wear out. Also, as you grow in skill, you may outgrow your present machine. If you find yourself in the market for a new machine, consider an upgrade.

Needles

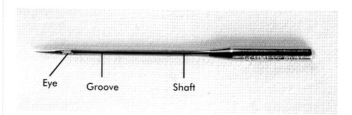

Eye   Groove   Shaft

There are numerous brands and varieties of needles to choose from. It is easy to become confused and overwhelmed. Not to worry! We will focus on the needs of the beginning machine quilter working with cotton fabric and 100% cotton or polyester thread.

Probably the most important consideration is that your needle and thread are compatible. If you use a higher-end needle and good-quality thread, you're halfway home.

Machine needles come in various sizes; the higher the number, the larger the needle (that is, the wider the shaft).

Needles marketed as machine quilting needles are sharps. A size 90/14 is a good choice to start with. As you improve, you may wish to move to a finer needle (a size 75/11, for example). A finer needle makes smaller holes, and the stitching appears more precise.

Choose a needle with an eye that is wide enough so it doesn't shred the thread. For this reason, some quilters prefer a denim sharp, which has a bigger eye. Save topstitching needles—which also have a large eye, as well as a deeper groove—for use with metallic and decorative threads.

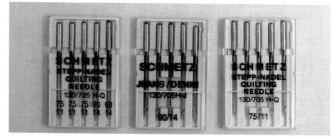

A variety of sharps for machine quilting

Troubleshooting for Needles

If...

you have been sewing for six to eight hours, or

you are beginning a new project, or

you hear a dull punching sound when the needle goes through the fabric

then...

change to a fresh needle.

If...

your thread shreds

then...

the eye of the needle is probably too small. Change to a needle with a larger eye (a denim sharp, for example).

If...

you are removing the needles from their packaging and need to remember which is which

then...

label the sections of a tomato pincushion and use it for easy storage and identification.

If...

you have used needles to dispose of but are concerned about safety

then...

use an ice pick or awl (carefully!) to make a hole in the top of an empty pill container and drop the spent needles inside.

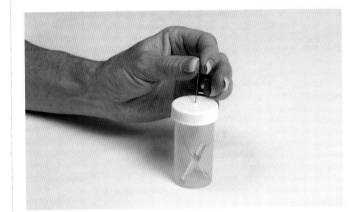

Threads

With so many delicious threads available on the market, it's impossible to expect your local quilt shop to carry them all, but your shop is likely to carry the basics to get you started.

Things have changed since you took home economics class in junior high school…or possibly even since you took your first quilting class. Higher-end polyester threads have entered the twenty-first century. Matching the fiber of the thread to the fiber of the fabric is no longer necessary. Did you know that the newer home sewing machines are calibrated for polyester threads? As a result, you will want to focus on either a cotton or a polyester thread for your initial machine quilting experiences. Save the metallic and other decorative threads for later, when you have more quilting mileage under your belt.

tip Do research! The Internet is a great source for exploring the options for both threads and needles. See Resources (page 54).

Thread comes in various weights, and the weight is indicated by a number on the spool. The higher the number, the finer the thread; so, for example, a 60-weight thread is finer than a 40-weight thread. A natural place to start would be somewhere in the middle—a 50-weight thread—which, coincidentally, is a good match for our recommended 90/14 needle!

tip Here's a good rule of thumb for helping you choose which thread weight and color to use. If you want your stitches to show dramatically, use a heavier thread (30- or 40-weight) in a contrasting color. If you want your stitches to blend into the background, use a finer thread (60- or 70-weight) in a matching color. Just remember to change the needle to match the thread weight.

Sample stitched with heavier, 40-weight variegated thread

Sample stitched with medium, 50-weight thread in a slightly contrasting color

Sample stitched with finer, 60-weight matching thread

If you've been tuned in to machine quilting at all, you've probably heard about monofilament thread. Monofilament is used when you want the machine quilting to be virtually invisible on the surface of the quilt. It comes both in clear and in a smoky gray color that disappears into darker fabrics.

Clear and smoky monofilament thread

Monofilament can be either nylon or polyester. I highly recommend that you stick with the polyester product. Nylon can stretch or become brittle with age. Be wary of products labeled as polyamide. Although the term "polyamide" sounds like "polyester," the former is a nylon product and not best suited to your quilting needs.

Marking Tools

A water-soluble pen is often my first choice to mark my quilts for machine quilting (although I avoid this type of pen for hand quilting—where it may leave a residue that can be tough to quilt through). Be aware that there are rules for playing with this type of pen. Follow the manufacturer's instructions *carefully*. You must also be willing and able to immerse the finished quilt in cold water to remove the markings.

Another option for marking—particularly on darker fabrics—is a silver Verithin pencil. This is an easy-to-see, easy-to-sharpen marking tool, and the marks come out with a gentle washing. Formerly available only at art and office supply stores, this pencil has become a staple at many quilt shops.

Samples of suitable marking tools

Chalk is less than ideal for marking quilts for machine quilting because it tends to rub off before the quilting process is complete. I also strongly advise against using a standard no. 2 pencil. In my experience, the soft lead simply won't come out.

That brings me to another, very important recommendation. No matter which marking tool you are planning to use, *always test it first* on the fabric you intend to mark. If the lines are difficult to see, or cannot be removed easily, choose a different marking tool.

Gloves and Other Goodies

There are many tools available to help with the free-motion quilting process (page 24). All are designed to give you a better grip on and more control of the quilt sandwich as you stitch, therefore improving your ergonomics and easing the tension in your body (hands and shoulders). These tools include specially made gloves, foam paddles, stickum for your hands, and finger cots. Note that these tools are not generally intended for use with a walking foot, because when you use a walking foot, the feed dogs, rather than you, move the quilt sandwich.

Samples of helpful notions for free-motion quilting

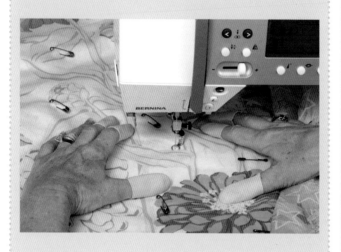

tip Try this trick I learned from noted machine quilter Sue Nickels; it's become my favorite. Find a pair of dishwashing gloves that fit snugly. (The dollar or variety store is a good source.) Cut the fingers off the gloves and place the glove fingers on the thumb, pointer, and middle fingers of each hand. Presto! Instant control!

Checklist for Machine Quilting Equipment

- Suitable sewing machine

- Walking foot (straight-line quilting) or darning foot (free-motion quilting)

- 90/14 sharp needle

- 50-weight 100% cotton (or polyester) thread

- Water-soluble marker, silver Verithin pencil, or both, for marking

- Gloves or other item for controlling the fabric as you stitch

- 100% cotton batting

- Size no. 1 safety pins for basting

Batting and Pins for Basting

I recommend 100% cotton batting, or at least 80% cotton, for machine quilting. The cotton fabric in the quilt top and backing clings to the cotton in the batting, and the clinging, accompanied by proper basting, greatly reduces shifting in the layers as you quilt. Cotton is also sturdy and stands up to the rigors of the machine quilting process. (Polyester can be stretchy.) Be sure to read the manufacturer's instructions for any preparation required for the batting you choose.

Cut the batting slightly larger—at least 2″ larger on all sides—than the quilt top.

Use safety pins for basting. You can remove them easily as you come to them. You don't need anything fancy (such as bent pins); just avoid anything that is too large. Rustproof size no. 1 pins are a good choice. The colored ones are extremely pliable, easy to see…and fun!

Preparing the Environment

Your Physical Setup

For machine quilting, as with all machine sewing, you want to be as comfortable as possible. I can't stress this enough! When I had the delicious opportunity to take a class from master machine quilter Diane Gaudynski, I realized how important the physical setup for machine quilting really is. It was in her class that I discovered that my usual setup was fine for piecing but placed ten strikes against me for machine quilting: it was the wrong height and provided no support for the weight of the quilt. No wonder I was frustrated and exhausted by the process!

Here are some of the things I consider essential to machine quilting success.

Table of the right height! You'll want to be able to sit with your elbows and knees bent at a 45° angle. Any other angle will place unnecessary strain on your neck, wrists, elbows, and knees. Position the table so the quilt can't fall off the edge: against a wall or in a corner, for example. If this is not possible, try surrounding the end of the table with chairs to help support the quilt's weight. Another option would be to set up your ironing board at the left side of the table; adjust the board to the table's height to best support the weight of the quilt.

Your sewing machine dealer will probably introduce you to a variety of specially designed, commercially manufactured sewing tables, if you haven't discovered them already. My advice is to take a little time to explore machine quilting to see whether you enjoy the process. If you do (and I think you will!), I strongly suspect a specially designed sewing table is in your future.

Slide-on acrylic tray. This device extends the bed of your sewing machine, giving you an enlarged surface for machine quilting. (You'll find it useful for piecing too.) It is a great way to adapt your machine for use on a regular table.

Look for a sturdy, well-constructed unit that aligns perfectly with the bed of your machine.

Adjustable office chair. For maximum flexibility, you'll want an armless chair that swivels and adjusts in height.

Lighting. Don't underestimate the importance of good lighting! The overhead lighting in your sewing space is probably not sufficient; supplement it with a portable light that you can adjust and direct where the light is most needed. Position it so there is no glare and so it doesn't cast any shadows.

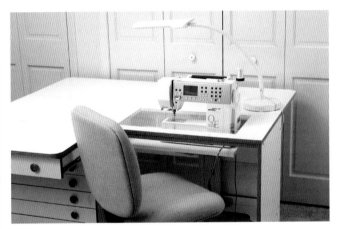

The ideal machine-quilting setup

An adapted setup

Mental Preparation: Things That Go Bump in the Night

You are set to go. You have your quilt marked and basted. Your physical setup is right on the money, and your favorite tunes float through the air. But something is missing. The key ingredient? Your mental attitude. *Yes*, that's right! Even with the best sewing machine on the market coupled with the best setup, it all comes down to *you*!

When I was a little girl, I had to make sure my closet door was shut tight at bedtime because that was when the big smiling green alligators wearing Mardi Gras beads came out to dance on their hind legs. I smile thinking of this memory, because the alligators were as real as real could be for a little girl tucked in her bed. I wonder now why I didn't get up and dance with them…

What does this memory have to do with mental attitude, you might ask? As I mentioned in the Introduction (page 4), my decision to conquer machine quilting also came at night. After much fear and procrastination, I realized that there was no reason I couldn't learn to dance. After all, in my sewing room I had two top-of-the-line Bernina sewing machines ready and waiting to sew. At that moment, I realized my negative attitude about machine quilting was all in my head. I had turned the mental corner. When it was time to get up the next morning, my thoughts were filled not with dread but with anticipation and excitement. I was going to learn a new skill…and become good at it. Was it a slam dunk when I sat at the machine and began quilting? No, but the process became one of joy and understanding…and I love it. I encourage you also to approach the process with a sense of wonder and excitement. If you find your shoulders up to your ears, walk around the room and shake off any tension. Just as with the dancing alligators in a little girl's bedroom, there is nothing to be scared of!

Preparing the Quilt

Now that your quilt top is finished, press it carefully. Proper pressing can determine the success of your machine quilting.

tip As you press the finished quilt top in preparation for basting, make sure there are no "flop overs" (that is, seam allowances that change sides midseam). This will make it easier to quilt in the ditch when you anchor the quilt later (page 19).

Marking

Unless you are planning to do free-form meander quilting, also called stipple quilting (page 26), I recommend that you mark the entire quilt—even straight lines—from the center outward before sitting down at your machine. That way, when you begin to sew, you can focus on and enjoy the stitching process. See Marking Tools (page 9) for recommended marking tools.

You can mark the top of the quilt using commercially available templates, or use the patterns provided in this book, which were designed specifically for each project, to make your own templates. Note that the lines in these patterns are continuous whenever possible, minimizing the number of starts and stops you'll need to make. However, some of the patterns do provide places to practice your "go-overs," that is, areas of double stitching (page 16).

You can also trace the patterns in this book (or patterns from other books or magazines) directly onto the quilt top. A light source behind the pattern makes the design easier to see. You can tape the quilt top to a window (if the quilt is small enough), use a lightbox, adapt a glass-topped dining or coffee table by placing a lamp beneath it, or create your own backlit surface with a ¼"-thick piece of Plexiglas (approximately 18" × 48"), two chairs, and a flashlight or lamp.

Adapting Designs for Machine Quilting

Many traditional quilting patterns and stencils are noncontinuous motifs. That means they involve numerous "unders and overs" (or broken lines) that require you to stop and start stitching...fussy and time-consuming for machine quilting.

Many of these patterns can easily be adapted for machine quilting. Study a pattern to see whether it is possible to connect the breaks and still maintain the sense of the design. The cable below is a good example. The version on the left is a traditional, noncontinuous cable. By connecting the "unders and overs," as in the version on the right, you can make the quilting lines continuous and turn this into an easy motif for machine quilting.

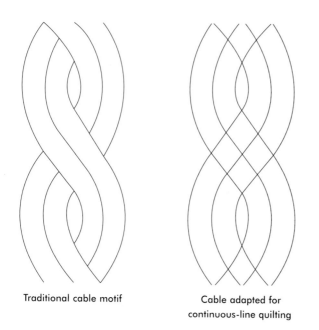

Traditional cable motif   Cable adapted for continuous-line quilting

It's not a good idea to leave any marking on your quilt for an extended time, so try not to mark too long before you intend to start quilting. Also, once your quilt is marked, don't expose it to heat, direct sunlight, or the iron, all of which can make the markings difficult to remove later.

Basting

As my first machine-quilting teacher, Margaret Gair, told me, it's all about the basting! Any shortcomings at the basting stage will only multiply as you move on through the quilting process. Do not skimp: the care you put into the basting will bear strongly on the final outcome of your quilting efforts.

Once the top is marked, I most often baste my quilts by spreading the layers flat on the floor. Think of this process as quilting yoga. You may be a little stiff in the morning, but the results—a beautifully flat and square quilt—are worth the little aches and pains!

1. Cut (and piece, if necessary) a backing that is 2″–3″ larger than the quilt top on all sides. Press the backing. Spread the backing right side down on the floor; if you have carpet, make sure it is nonloop. Pull the backing taut but not tight and affix the edges to the floor every 2″ or so with T pins (for carpet) or masking tape (for bare flooring).

2. Prepare, according to the manufacturer's instructions, a batting that is at least 2″ larger than the quilt top on all sides. Center the batting over the backing (wrong side up).

3. Center the quilt top (right side up) over the batting and backing.

4. Use a large ruler to straighten and square the quilt, beginning with the outer border. Use the straightened outer-border seams as a guide for straightening the position of any long vertical and horizontal seams in the interior of the quilt.

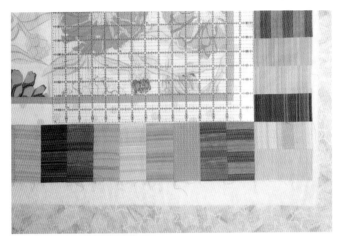

5. Working in quadrants from the center out, secure the three layers together with safety pins placed every 3″ (see page 10). Try not to place the pins where you will quilt over them. Pin-baste all the way to the edges of the quilt, but don't close the pins yet.

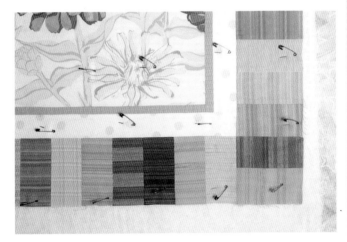

6. Release the quilt from the floor. Working carefully with the quilt in your lap, close the safety pins.

tip If you are not able to (or prefer not to) baste on the floor, you can use a large tabletop instead. You probably don't want to do this on your dining room table—the pins may scratch—but there are alternatives. Just be sure that whatever surface you use is clean and smooth and that you raise it as needed to spare your back.

- A ping-pong table with the net removed makes a great basting surface.

- Check with your church, library, or quilt shop. All may have large tables you can push together to use as a single large surface, and probably have the space for you to do so.

- Some quilters keep a collapsible worktable in their workspace for cutting fabric. These tables work well for basting too, especially the waist-high variety made especially for sewers.

Getting Started

Adjusting the Tension

As you get ready to machine quilt, you'll want to make sure the tension on your sewing machine is set correctly. Ideally, you want *just a speck* of bobbin thread to show on the top of your quilt and *just a speck* of top thread to show on the back. If you see anything more, your tension needs to be adjusted.

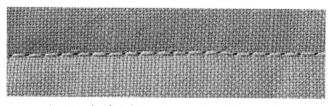

An example of stitching with properly adjusted tension

If you can see more than a speck of bobbin thread on the front of your quilt, you need to *loosen* the top tension, that is, change the setting to a *lower* number. More than a speck of top thread showing on the back of the quilt is a sign you need to *tighten* the top tension, or change the setting to a *higher* number.

It's always a good idea to make a small sample quilt sandwich using the fabric and batting you plan to use in your quilt. Practice machine quilting on the sample using the needle and thread you plan to use for your project. Adjust the tension on your machine as needed. Begin at your machine's normal or automatic tension setting and then make slight adjustments, testing as you go. When you've found the proper setting, make note of the materials and tension setting in a small notebook you keep just for this purpose. If you record the specifics, you'll have them on hand if your work on the project gets interrupted for an extended period of time—for example, by other sewing tasks—and the settings will also be available for future projects using similar materials.

Planning a Stitching Strategy

When you are machine quilting, you'll want to make as few stops and starts as possible, so look carefully at the motifs you intend to stitch and plan a stitching strategy before you begin. You may find it helpful to plot out your plan on a piece of paper in advance.

Assess the motifs you plan to use for obvious stopping and starting places so you can minimize these as much as possible. Determine whether there are areas that you can stitch over without drawing attention to the double stitching. (I call these areas "go-overs.") If there aren't any such areas, look for ways to adapt the motif; for example, create lines of side-by-side stitching that allow you to stitch continuously but still maintain—perhaps even enhance—the original design.

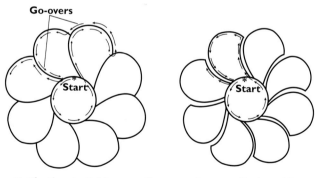

Motif with potential "go-overs"

Same motif adapted for continuous stitching with side-by-side stitching

You'll find more on specific stitching strategies in Anchoring (page 19), Straight-Line Quilting (page 22), and Simple-Curve Quilting (page 23).

tip As with hand quilting, you will want a consistent amount of stitching over the surface of the quilt; otherwise, the quilt will pooch out in places or wave at you from the edges—neither is a very attractive prospect!

Uneven amount of quilting

Consistent amount of quilting

Handling Bulk

One of the challenges all machine quilters eventually face is how to handle the bulk of the quilt at the sewing machine. The larger the quilt, the more bulk you will have to cope with. (It is with large quilts that you'll discover the importance of careful and thorough basting and a suitable physical setup!)

There are many techniques you can use to bundle or package your quilt. Experiment a bit to find the one that suits you best. I've kept the projects in this book relatively small to ease the learning curve. Once you feel confident handling these projects under the needle, you'll be ready to move on to much larger pieces.

I like to quilt my quilts from the center out, one half at a time, to make sure I don't quilt any bubbles (or mountains!) into the center. This strategy also ensures that I never have more than half of the quilt between the needle and the machine. I also find that quilting from the center out makes it easier to manipulate the quilt, which tends to become stiffer and less pliable as it is quilted.

1. Spread your quilt out flat. Roll the right edge of the quilt evenly toward the center, stopping a few inches from where you intend to place the first line of quilting.

2. If necessary, either roll or accordion pleat the left side of the quilt as well. If the table surface is large or the quilt is small enough, you may be able to simply arrange the left edge of the quilt on the surface. Just be sure the weight of the quilt is distributed evenly.

3. Take the quilt to your sewing machine. Outfit your machine with the proper foot and needle (page 6) and thread it with the appropriate thread (page 8). Make sure the presser foot is raised and the needle is in its highest position. Position the quilt so the rolled right edge is under the arm, the area you've left free is under the needle, and the rolled, pleated, or otherwise-arranged left edge is supported on your work surface to the left of the machine. You are ready to begin!

Right side of quilt is rolled.

Machine quilter Paula Reid uses a bundling method she calls "stuff and fluff" and has made a DVD that demonstrates her technique. See Resources (page 54) for additional information.

Starting and Stopping

Now that we've covered the preliminaries, it's time to sit down at your sewing machine and get started.

Starting

1. Reduce your stitch length almost (but not exactly) to 0 and lower the presser foot right over the spot where you plan to start quilting. Holding onto the top thread, take 1 complete stitch, so that the needle returns to its highest position.

2. Without raising the presser foot, gently tug the top thread to pull the loop of bobbin thread to the quilt surface. Pull the end of the bobbin thread through to the top.

Take 1 complete stitch; ending with needle at highest position.

Pull top thread to bring loop of bobbin thread to surface.

3. Insert the needle into the exact spot where the bobbin thread came up. Drop the feed dogs for free-motion quillting. Hold the threads to the side as you take 1 or 2 stitches.

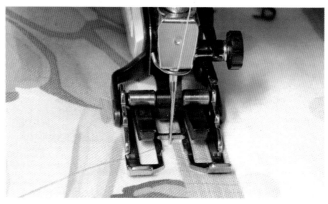

Insert needle and take 1 or 2 stitches.

4. Gradually increase the stitches to full length (approximately 10–12 stitches per inch) within 6–8 stitches. You're on your way!

Stopping

The process of stopping is the reverse of the process you used for starting. As you get within 6–8 stitches of a planned stopping point, gradually decrease the stitch length. Then drop the stitch length almost (but not exactly) to 0 and take 1 or 2 stitches. Lift the presser foot and gently pull the quilt away from the machine. Cut both the top thread and the bobbin thread, leaving a nice long tail on each.

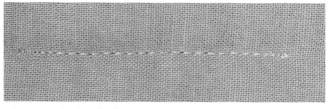

Transition the length of your stitches to begin and end your quilting.

Dealing with Thread Tails

There are two options for coping with the thread tails at the starting and stopping points of your machine quilting. My preference for eliminating thread tails is to pull the tail away from the quilt and use small, sharp embroidery scissors or thread clippers to *slice*—not clip—the thread as closely as possible to the quilt surface. The tiny stitches you took at the starting and stopping points will secure the threads. By slicing in a sideways and slightly upward motion, you avoid the possibility of accidentally cutting into the quilt. (Don't forget to clean up the back of the quilt as well.)

Slice, don't clip, the thread tails.

tip Some machine quilters prefer to tie off and bury the thread tails. If you choose this method, remove the quilt from the machine. Cut the threads, leaving enough length to tie and bury the knots. Pull the bobbin thread to the top by gently tugging on the top thread. Thread the tails onto a hand quilting needle and make a knot close to the surface of the quilt. Insert the needle into the top two layers of the sandwich right at the point where the stitching begins or ends. Run the needle between the layers for an inch or two and then bring it back to the surface and give it a gentle tug until you hear the knot pop between the layers. Trim the remaining tail as described above.

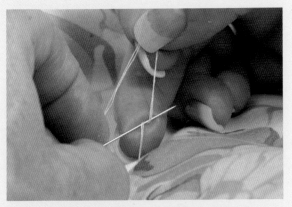

Make a knot close to the surface of the quilt.

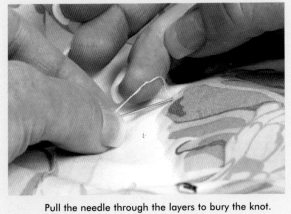

Pull the needle through the layers to bury the knot.

Whichever method you choose, you can do your clean up each time you stop, or you can wait until you have finished an entire section before going back for clean up. If you choose the latter, be careful not to catch the tails in your subsequent stitching.

Anchoring

Before you begin quilting any motifs or background filler, anchor the key seams in your quilt—by stitching between the rows of blocks, sashing, and borders on the side with less bulk (side without seam allowances). It's important that you get as close to the seam as possible. Be careful because the pressed seam allowances can jump from one side to the other between the blocks and sashing in the long seams, and you want your anchoring to be as straight and invisible as possible. (This procedure is called stitching in the ditch.)

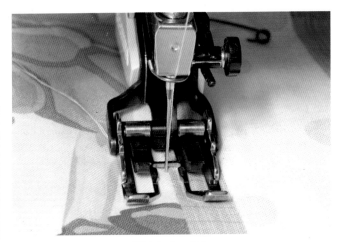

Stitch in the ditch.

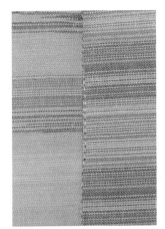

An example of poorly executed stitching in the ditch

An example of properly done, well-hidden stitching in the ditch

Stitching in the ditch supplements the basting and helps to keep the layers secure as you add the more decorative stitching.

1. Outfit your machine with the walking foot. Beginning at an edge, stitch the centermost long vertical (or diagonal) seam. Next, quilt all vertical (or diagonal) seams to the right of this centerline. Rotate the quilt from top to bottom, roll the other side of the quilt to fit under the sewing machine arm, and quilt the vertical (or diagonal) seams on the other side of the centerline.

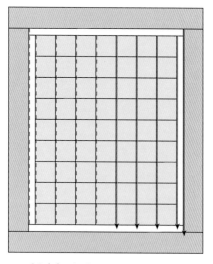

Stitch beginning at centermost seam.

2. Rotate your quilt, roll it where necessary, and quilt the centermost horizontal (or opposite diagonal) long seam of the quilt. Quilt first on one side of the centerline and then on the other side, as you did in Step 1.

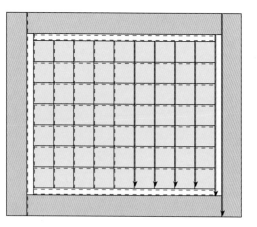

Remember to sew as close to the seam as you can, stitching along the side of the seam that is free of pressed seam allowances.

tip *Help keep your anchoring stitches out of sight: match the thread color to the color of the quilt top.*

Troubleshooting for Stops, Starts, and Tension

If…

the thread clumps or snarls when you take the first few machine quilting stitches

then…

you may have forgotten to hold the top and bottom threads while taking the first few stitches, or

you may have set your starting stitch length too low. You want to set it almost—but not quite—to 0.

If…

you see more than just a speck of bobbin thread on the top of your quilt or top thread on the quilt back

then…

the tension on your machine needs adjustment (page 16).

If…

your quilt is being puckered or pulled while you are stitching

then…

stop stitching!

The quilt may be hung up under your chair or on the corner of the table, or

the thread may be catching underneath the quilt, in which case you'll want to stop, tie off, and check the bobbin before proceeding.

Techniques and Practice Exercises

Stitch consistency is a primary goal for machine quilting, just as with hand quilting. There is one way to get there: master the fundamentals and practice, practice, practice!

Even though I now have confidence in my ability, I make it a practice to warm up before beginning (or resuming) any session of machine quilting. Warming up puts both my body and my mind in the right place. I encourage you to do this, too.

Make yourself a small practice sandwich using muslin for the quilt top and the same type of batting and backing that you will use in your quilt. This sandwich can double as the vehicle for testing and adjusting the machine tension (page 16). Remember: You can't jump from project to project and assume the settings will stay the same. Fabric, batting, needle, and thread all affect the tension setting.

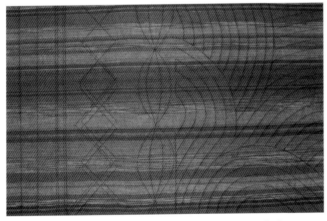

My sample sandwich with examples of various straight-line and simple-curve quilting motifs

One of the biggest mistakes new machine quilters make is trying to go *too fast*. Just because you are quilting by machine doesn't mean you must finish the quilt yesterday. Keep the pace slow and methodical—you are sewing, not riding Seabiscuit! Machine quilting can be a repetitive, meditative activity—probably slower in pace than you might think—so relax and enjoy it.

This next tip will be a tough one, but train yourself *not* to look at the needle as you stitch. Look an inch or so ahead of the needle to anticipate where you are going, rather than where you are or have already been. Looking ahead prepares you to react, keeping you both relaxed and in control. The needle *will* go up and down even if you aren't looking at it—I promise!

When you need to stop and reposition either the quilt sandwich or your hands, always stop and restart in the same needle hole. This is where both the knee lift and needle up/needle down functions will prove extremely helpful. When you foresee an adjustment, try to make the transition in an area where the thread color matches the fabric so the transition will be invisible.

tip Position your hands on the quilt sandwich in such a way as to maximize the area you can stitch before you'll need to reposition them, but not so far apart that you are uncomfortable or you lose control of the sandwich.

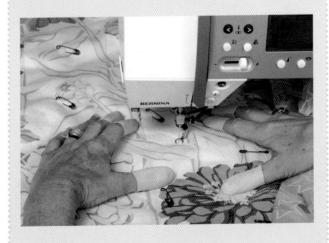

Finally, be kind to your body. Occasionally pause, raise your head, and gaze softly into the distance to relax your eyes. Stop for a stretch every twenty minutes or so. Gently move your head in small circles and lower your ear to your shoulder. Raise and lower your shoulders to keep them loose. If you are feeling especially tense, take a more extended break. Go for a walk, work in the garden, have a cup of tea. You'll come back to the sewing machine feeling refreshed and ready to go again.

Straight-Line Quilting

Straight-line quilting includes any quilting that is—surprise! —stitched in straight lines. This includes anchoring (page 19) and other stitch-in-the-ditch quilting, outline quilting geometric shapes within blocks and borders, and quilting single or parallel straight or diagonal lines and grids.

Detail of *Scrappy Nine Patch* (page 37)

Straight lines can be tricky. (Have you ever tried to draw a straight line without a ruler?) Many machine quilters use a walking foot (also referred to as an even-feed foot) with the feed dogs up for straight-line quilting (page 6). The walking foot guides the multiple layers of fabric through the machine evenly, minimizing the chance for shifting and puckers. In the beginning, you'll want to use your walking foot for straight-line quilting. Once you have mastered free-motion quilting, however, you may find that you prefer to do your straight-line quilting free-motion (page 24) as well, to avoid having to turn the quilt to change direction.

I did the straight-line quilting for *Straight Furrows* (page 44) free-motion. If I had had to turn the quilt for every change of direction, I'd still be quilting!

Some walking feet, particularly the newer ones, come with a built-in guide that rides along the previous line of stitching and helps you stitch evenly spaced parallel lines. If you have one of these feet, you may find you can skip marking, particularly for smaller areas such as block backgrounds or borders. (Personally, I prefer to mark.)

As with all machine quilting, take it slowly when straight-line quilting. Don't pull on the quilt; let the walking foot and the feed dogs do most of the work. For large areas, quilt parallel lines, grids, and other crosshatched designs using the top-to-bottom, side-to-side strategy described for anchoring (page 19). Ending each line of stitching at the bottom and then beginning again anew at the top may seem tedious, but doing so will allow you to stitch large sections without turning the quilt—an advantage you will come to appreciate quickly!

tip Always plan a quilting strategy. Sometimes drawing little arrows along with your pattern will help you get comfortable with the process.

EXERCISE #1

Make up an approximately 18″ × 24″ sample sandwich for practice. Begin by marking and quilting straight lines; then move on to evenly spaced pairs of double straight lines spaced ⅛″–¼″ apart. (Doubling the lines adds incredible texture to the finished quilt.)

EXERCISE #2

Next, experiment with an overall gridded design. If your walking foot has a guide, familiarize yourself with how it works.

Examples of overall gridded designs

Simple-Curve Quilting

Many simple curves can also be machine quilted using the walking foot with the feed dogs up (curved lines, cables, fans, and so on). These gentle curves make a nice substitute for grids and other overall straight-line designs on the surface of a strongly geometric pieced quilt.

Border detail of *Floral Fiesta* (page 31)

EXERCISE #3

Use your marking tool to draw some soft curves on your sample sandwich. There are some good examples in my sample (page 21) and the illustrations below. Stitch the marked curves and, when you feel comfortable, try stitching some curves without marking them first.

Mark, then stitch.

Echo quilt.

Free-Motion Quilting

Free-motion quilting is the best method for quilting cables and wreaths, stipple quilting, echo quilting around appliqués, and other patterns that require lots of curves and changes of direction. With free-motion quilting, you—rather than the machine—move the fabric under the needle and guide the direction of the stitching *without having to turn the quilt.* Most quilters accomplish this by using a darning foot and dropping the feed dogs on the machine. Others—myself included—have had success leaving the feed dogs up, depending upon how tight the curves are and how complex the motif is. I encourage you to try both ways to see which method you prefer.

On one thing most quilters agree—use the darning foot for free-motion stitching (see page 6). There are basically two types of darning feet to consider as you begin your machine-quilting journey: open toe and closed toe. I prefer the open toe to the closed toe because the former allows greater visibility as I stitch; however, the closed toe will work just fine.

My sample sandwich with examples of meandering, free-form flowers, a simple motif, and, of course, my signature

EXERCISE #4

Let's start off simple. Again, you will need a sample sandwich (about 18″ × 24″) for practice. This time outfit your machine with the darning foot. Before layering the three layers of your sandwich, choose a simple motif such as the one in the outer corner of *Basket in Blue* (on the pullout). Mark the motif off to one side of the sample. Start stitching to get the feel and motion of the process. Doodle, just like you did when you were a kid. Try your hand at meandering —then how about a chain of small flowers? Gradually work your way over to the motif and see how closely you can stay on the lines. Finish with your signature—after all, this is your first thread painting!

Detail of *Basket in Blue* (page 48)

tip Stitching the area around a motif such as a flower or cable (sometimes called filler quilting) causes unstitched areas to pop forward, increasing their importance in the design. Filler quilting also adds a luxurious layer of texture to the quilt. Be sure to balance the size of the motif with the scale of the background quilting, so the primary motif doesn't pooch.

Motif with no background quilting

Motif with gridded background

Following the Fabric Motif

Following a fabric motif is a super-easy way to practice free-motion quilting. It requires no marking, and slight wobbles or variations in the stitching will be hidden in the fabric print. It is also a wonderful way to experiment with different thread types and colors. The large center panel of *Floral Fiesta* (page 31) demonstrates this technique.

EXERCISE #5

To practice, make a small quilt sandwich using a large-scale print fabric as the top layer and then simply follow all or part of the outline of any large-scale motif in the printed fabric.

Detail of *Floral Fiesta* (page 31)

A close cousin to this technique is echo quilting. With this method, you stitch around an appliqué shape, first right along its outside edge, then ⅛″ to ¼″ further outward. Continue outlining the shape, moving outward with consistently spaced bands of stitching, until you reach the outer limits of the block or meet another area of quilting.

An example of echo quilting

Quilting a Complex Motif

Motifs such as cables and feathered wreaths are more complex and take a bit more time to master. For example, gently curved cables may look easy, but the curves must stay evenly spaced and flow in unison. This is not to say you can't machine quilt them! As always, all it takes is practice.

Border detail of *Scrappy Nine Patch* (page 37)

EXERCISE #6

Set yourself up with a sample quilt sandwich and use the same methods you used to practice quilting a simple motif (page 24), this time with the cable pattern on the pullout page. When you've mastered that, try the wreath on the pullout.

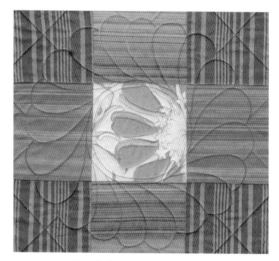

Detail of Placemat 4 (page 28)

Stipple Quilting

Sometimes called meandering or meander quilting, stipple quilting follows no pattern, but wanders over the quilt surface in a maze of curving lines. It works beautifully as filler behind appliqué motifs and stands equally well on its own. The curves resemble the interlocking edges of jigsaw puzzle pieces. In traditional stippling, the curving lines never cross. Most quilters do not mark stippled designs, but quilt them free-form instead.

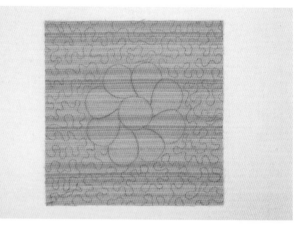

Example of properly planned and executed stipple quilting

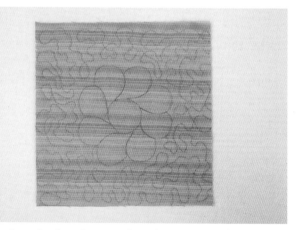

Example of poorly executed stipple quilting. The lines should be more evenly spaced and never cross.

EXERCISE #7

Practice drawing stipple designs on paper first so you can become accustomed to the movement of the design. Study your drawings to determine a starting and ending strategy. Once you feel comfortable, you are ready to practice on a sample sandwich. It's okay to start stitching off the quilt top or bump out to the edge again if you find yourself caught in a stippling maze.

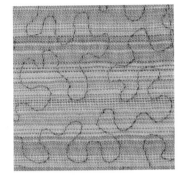

Warm-Up Exercise

Make yourself a small practice sandwich using muslin for the quilt top and the same type of batting and backing that you will use in your quilt.

Turn on some good music—whatever helps you to relax or takes you to a spot that makes you happy. Listening to music is a wonderful way to aid the transition out of your linear left brain into your creative right brain.

Begin by quilting some straight lines; then do some doodles such as curlicues and stars. Try writing your name. As you begin to loosen up, experiment by "drawing" one of the motifs you intend to quilt. This experiment will give you confidence, as well as the opportunity to test your stitching strategy. I always do a prominent motif planned for the quilt as part of my warm-up before starting to quilt.

Sample warm-up exercise

Troubleshooting for Quilting

If...

your machine is skipping stitches

then...

your needle may be dull, burred, or bent; insert a new needle, or

the presser foot pressure may need adjustment. Check your machine manual for guidance.

If...

you are getting tucks and/or pleats on the back of the quilt

then...

you may not have basted properly or sufficiently; remove the quilt from the machine, return to your basting surface, and adjust as needed, or

you may need to change to the walking foot on your sewing machine.

If...

you feel like the sewing machine or the quilt is "driving" you, rather than vice versa

then...

stop, take a deep breath, and slow down. You are probably sewing too fast.

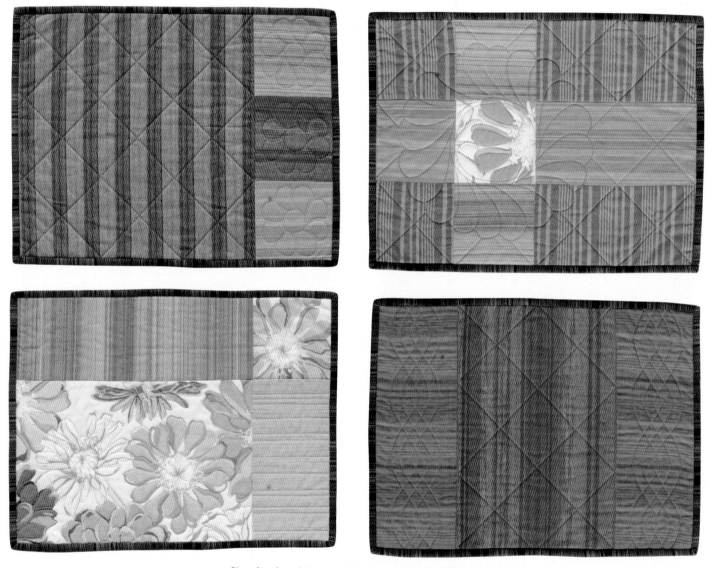

Pieced and machine quilted by Alex Anderson, 2006.

Finished placemat size: 16½″ × 12½″

Skill level: Beginner

These simple-to-piece placemats provide the perfect small canvases for trying out your newfound machine-quilting skills. Each placemat covers a different combination of basic techniques: straight lines and grids, following the fabric motif, curved flowers, wreaths (with go-overs), and continuous-line cables. You'll not only polish your skills but also end up with four colorful trimmings for the family table.

Materials

Fabric amounts are based on a 42″ fabric width.

Brightly colored, large-scale floral print: ⅓ yard for Placemats 1 and 4 (**Fabric A**)

Coordinating subtle stripes: Fat quarter each of 9 different fabrics for Placemats 1–4 (**Fabrics B1–B9**)

Dark coordinating subtle stripe: ⅝ yard for binding (**Fabric C**)

Backing: 1 yard

Batting: Four pieces 20″ × 16″

Cutting

All measurements include ¼″ seam allowances.

From the brightly colored, large-scale floral print (Fabric A)

Cut 1 piece 8½″ × 12½″.

Cut 2 squares 4½″ × 4½″.

From the coordinating subtle stripes (Fabrics B1–B9)

Cut 1 piece 4½″ × 12½″ (B1).

Cut 1 piece 4½″ × 8½″ (B2).

Cut 1 piece 8½″ × 12½″ (B3).

Cut 2 pieces 4½″ × 12½″ (B4).

Cut 3 squares 4½″ × 4½″ (B5).

Cut 1 square 4½″ × 4½″ (B6).

Cut 1 piece 4½″ × 8½″ (B7).

Cut 2 squares *each* 4½″ × 4½″ (B7 and B9).

Cut 1 square 12½″ × 12½″ (B8).

Cut 2 pieces 4½″ × 8½″ (B9).

From the dark coordinating stripe (Fabric C)

Cut 8 strips 2⅛″ × the fabric width.

From the backing fabric

Cut 2 strips 16″ × the fabric width; crosscut into 4 pieces 20″ × 16″.

Placemat 1

(Arrows indicate pressing direction.)

1. Sew the 4½″ × 12½″ Fabric B1 piece and the 8½″ × 12½″ Fabric A piece together. Press.

2. Sew one 4½″ Fabric A square and the 4½″ × 8½″ Fabric B2 piece together. Press.

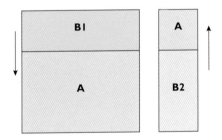

3. Sew the units from Steps 1 and 2 together. Press.

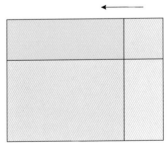

Placemat 1

Placemat 2

Sew the 8½″ × 12½″ Fabric B3 piece between the two 4½″ × 12½″ Fabric B4 pieces. Press.

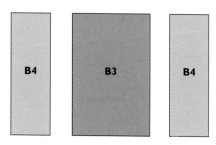

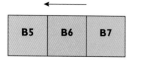

Placemat 2

Placemat 3

1. Sew three 4½″ Fabric B5, B6, and B7 squares together as shown. Press.

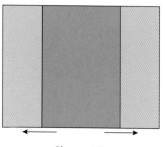

2. Sew the unit from Step 1 to the 12½″ Fabric B8 square. Press.

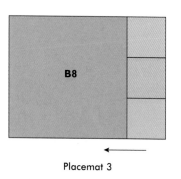

Placemat 3

Placemat 4

1. Sew one 4½″ Fabric B7 square between the two 4½″ Fabric B9 squares. Press.

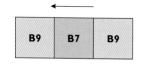

2. Sew one 4½″ Fabric A square between two 4½″ Fabric B5 squares. Press.

3. Sew the 4½″ × 8½″ Fabric B7 piece between the two 4½″ × 8½″ Fabric B9 pieces. Press.

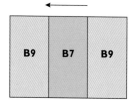

4. Arrange and sew the units from Steps 1–3. Press.

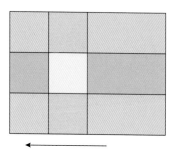

Placemat 4

Finishing

1. Refer to the diagrams below for suggested quilting motifs. Patterns appear on the pullout page.

2. Follow the instructions in Preparing the Quilt (pages 13–15) to mark, layer, and baste each placemat.

3. Machine quilt as desired.

4. Sew the 2⅛″-wide Fabric C strips together end to end with diagonal seams and press the seams open. Use this to bind the edges of the quilt; refer to Binding (page 52).

Suggested quilting motifs

Pieced and machine quilted by Alex Anderson, 2006.

Finished quilt size: 38½″ × 42½″

Skill level: Beginner

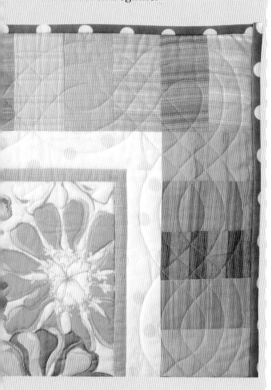

You'll learn a lot while quilting this festive little quilt. The large-scale floral fabric is ideal for polishing your free-motion skills—no need to mark; just outline the oversized blooms. (I changed the thread color to match each flower—not necessary, but fun!) Give yourself permission to cross the lines as I have by using a single large cable to span the two outermost borders. The cable on the pullout page is elongated, with curves that are gentle enough for a walking foot. To make the stitching even easier, I minimized stops and starts by adapting the "unders and overs" of the original for continuous-line quilting.

Materials

Fabric amounts are based on a 42″ fabric width.

Brightly colored, large-scale floral print: 1 yard for center panel (**Fabric A**)

Coordinating subtle geometric print: ¼ yard for inner border (**Fabric B**)

Coordinating polka dot print with white background: ⅜ yard for middle border (**Fabric C**)

Assorted coordinating subtle geometric prints: 1 yard *total* for pieced outer border (**Fabric D**)*

Blue polka dot print: ⅜ yard for binding (**Fabric E**)

Backing: 2½ yards

Batting: 43″ × 47″

* You may use Fabric B for one of these prints.

Cutting

All measurements include ¼″ seam allowances.

From the brightly colored, large-scale floral print (Fabric A)

Cut 1 piece 26½″ × 30½″.

From the coordinating subtle geometric print (Fabric B)

Cut 2 strips 1″ × 30½″.

Cut 2 strips 1″ × 27½″.

From the coordinating polka dot print with white background (Fabric C)

Cut 2 strips 2″ × 31½″.

Cut 2 strips 2″ × 30½″.

From the assorted coordinating subtle geometric prints (Fabric D)

Cut a *total* of 10 strips 2½″ × the fabric width.

Cut a *total* of 12 pieces 2½″ × 4½″.

Blue polka dot print (Fabric E)

Cut 5 strips 2⅛″ × the fabric width.

Quilt Assembly

(Arrows indicate pressing direction.)

1. Sew the 1″ × 30½″ Fabric B strips to opposite sides of the 26½″ × 30½″ Fabric A piece. Press. Sew the 1″ × 27½″ Fabric B strips to the top and bottom of the quilt. Press.

2. Sew the 2″ × 31½″ Fabric C strips to the sides of the unit from Step 1 and then sew the 2″ × 30½″ Fabric C strips to the top and bottom of the quilt. Press.

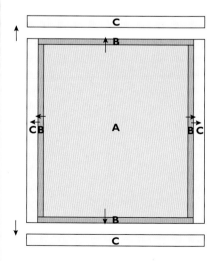

3. Arrange and sew 5 assorted 2½″ Fabric D strips together to make a scrappy strip set. Press. Make another scrappy strip set. Cut the strip sets into segments 4½″ wide. You'll use 12 of these.

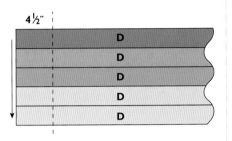

Make 2 strip sets.
Cut 12 segments.

4. Sew 3 scrappy segments from Step 3 together to make an outer border. Press. Make a total of 4 borders.

Make 4.

5. Sew 1 border from Step 4 to the top of the unit from Step 2 and 1 border to the bottom. Press.

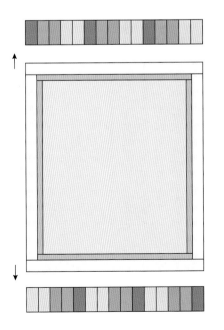

6. Sew 2 assorted 2½″ × 4½″ Fabric D pieces together. Press. Make 6 of these units.

Make 6.

7. Arrange and sew 3 units from Step 6 to each remaining border from Step 4. Refer to the photo (page 31) and the illustration below, carefully turning the small units. Press. Sew the resulting borders to the sides of the quilt. Press.

Finishing

1. Refer to the diagram below for suggested quilting motifs. The cable pattern appears on the pullout page.

2. Follow the instructions in Preparing the Quilt (pages 13–15) to mark, layer, and baste your quilt.

3. Machine quilt as desired.

4. Sew the 2⅛″-wide Fabric E strips together end to end with diagonal seams and press the seams open. Use this to bind the edges of the quilt; refer to Binding (page 52).

Suggested quilting motifs

Pieced and machine quilted by Alex Anderson, 2006.

Finished quilt size: 46½" × 56½"

Finished block size: 3" × 6"

Number of blocks: 80

Skill level: Confident beginner

This quilt was inspired by the jazzy 1930s reproduction fabrics I had hanging around in my stash. I found the bright, fresh colors irresistible, and I think the red binding ties the whole piece together, don't you?

I love the look of crosshatched grids—a standard quilting treatment that has stood the test of time. I enjoy quilting them too, so I used this classic straight-line technique in the sashing and in the border. A gently curving cable—made continuous for machine quilting, of course!—flows through the pieced geese.

Materials

Fabric amounts are based on a 42" fabric width.

Assorted pastel solids: ½ yard *total* for blocks (**Fabric A**)

Assorted 1930s-style prints: 2⅜ yards *total* for blocks, pieced sashing, and pieced borders (**Fabric B**)

Off-white solid: 1 yard for blocks (**Fabric C**)

Red solid: ½ yard for binding (**Fabric D**)

Backing: 3 yards

Batting: 51" × 61"

Cutting

All measurements include ¼" seam allowances.

From the assorted pastel solids (Fabric A)

Cut a *total* of 40 squares 3" × 3"; cut each square in half once diagonally to make 2 half-square triangles (80 total).

From the assorted 1930s-style prints (Fabric B)

Cut a *total* of 40 squares 3" × 3"; cut each square in half once diagonally to make 2 half-square triangles (80 total).*

Cut a *total* of 40 squares 4¼" × 4¼"; cut each square in half twice diagonally to make 4 quarter-square triangles (160 total).*

Cut a *total* of 18 strips 2½" × the fabric width.

From the off-white solid (Fabric C)

Cut 8 strips 3⅞" × the fabric width; crosscut the strips into 80 squares 3⅞" × 3⅞"; cut each square in half once diagonally to make 2 half-square triangles (160 total).

From the red solid (Fabric D)

Cut 6 strips 2⅛" × the fabric width.

* Cut these in matching sets of one 3" × 3" square and one 4¼" × 4¼" square.

Making the Blocks

(Arrows indicate pressing direction.)

1. Sew a Fabric A half-square triangle right sides together with a Fabric B half-square triangle. Press. Make 80 of these units in 40 sets of matching pairs.

Make 80 in matching pairs.

2. Sew a matching Fabric B quarter-square triangle to adjacent sides of each unit from Step 1. Press. Make 80 of these units.

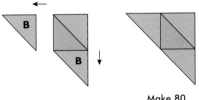

Make 80.

3. Sew a Fabric C triangle to the short sides of each unit from Step 2. Press. Make 80.

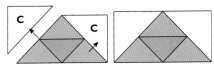

Make 80.

4. Sew 16 units from Step 3 together to make a vertical row. Press. Make 5 rows.

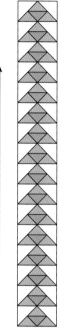

Make 5.

Quilt Assembly

1. Arrange and sew 6 assorted 2½"-wide Fabric B strips together to make a scrappy strip set. Press. Make 3 scrappy strip sets. Cut the strip sets into 48 segments 2½" wide.

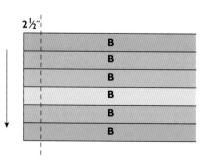

Make 3 strip sets. Cut 48 segments.

2. Sew 4 segments from Step 1 together. Press. Make 12.

Make 12.

3. Arrange the block rows and 8 of the units from Step 2 as shown in the assembly diagram. Sew the rows and units together. Press.

4. Remove 1 square from each remaining unit from Step 2. Sew 2 units together lengthwise. Press. Make 2.

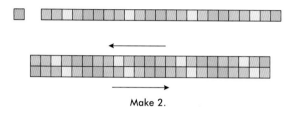

Make 2.

5. Sew a unit from Step 4 to the top and bottom of the quilt. Press.

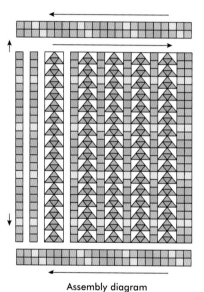

Assembly diagram

Suggested quilting motifs

Finishing

1. Refer to the diagram above for suggested quilting motifs. The cable pattern appears on the pullout page.

2. Follow the instructions in Preparing the Quilt (pages 13–15) to mark, layer, and baste your quilt.

3. Machine quilt as desired.

4. Sew the 2⅛"-wide Fabric D strips together end to end with diagonal seams and press the seams open. Use this to bind the edges of the quilt; refer to Binding (page 52).

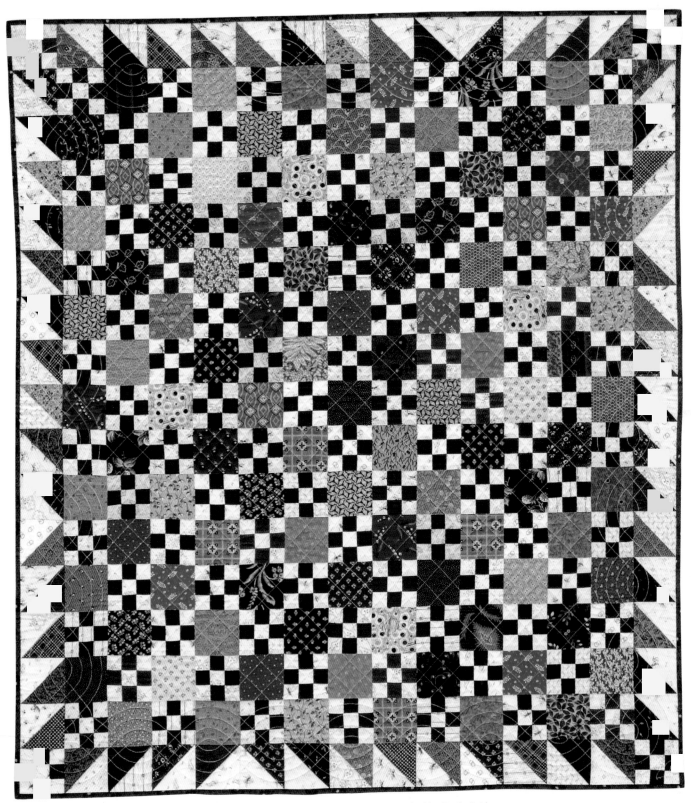

Pieced by Alex Anderson, 2004. Machine quilted by Paula Reid.

Finished quilt size: 45½″ × 51½″

Finished block size: 3″ × 3″

Number of Nine-Patch blocks: 102

Number of plain blocks: 97

Number of half-square triangle blocks: 56

Skill level: Confident beginner

Here's the *perfect* quilt to showcase the straight-line and continuous-curve quilting techniques you've just mastered.

This homey, traditional quilt lends itself beautifully to one of my favorite tried-and-true quilting motifs: the diagonal crosshatched grid. The simple overall design covers the center of the quilt, perfectly offsetting the strong vertical and horizontal lines of the pieced blocks. A chunky cable crosses the lines of the Sawtooth border, spilling playfully into the outermost rows of blocks.

Materials

Fabric amounts are based on a 42″ fabric width.

Assorted red solids: ⅞ yard *total* for Nine-Patch blocks (**Fabric A**)

Assorted light documentary prints: 1½ yards *total* for Nine-Patch blocks and Sawtooth border (**Fabric B**)

Assorted medium and dark documentary prints: 1½ yards *total* for plain blocks and Sawtooth border (**Fabric C**)

Dark brown documentary print: ½ yard for binding (**Fabric D**)

Backing: 3 yards

Batting: 50″ × 56″

Cutting

All measurements include ¼″ seam allowances.

From the assorted red solids (Fabric A)

Cut a *total* of 17 strips 1½″ × 20″.*

Cut a *total* of 34 strips 1½″ × 10″ in matching pairs.*

From the assorted light documentary prints (Fabric B)

Cut a *total* of 34 strips 1½″ × 20″ in matching pairs.**

Cut a *total* of 17 strips 1½″ × 10″.**

Cut a *total* of 28 squares 3⅞″ × 3⅞″; cut each square in half once diagonally to make 2 half-square triangles (56 total).

From the assorted medium and dark documentary prints (Fabric C)

Cut a *total* of 97 squares 3½″ × 3½″.

Cut a *total* of 28 squares 3⅞″ × 3⅞″; cut each square in half once diagonally to make 2 half-square triangles (56 total).

From the dark brown print (Fabric D)

Cut 6 strips 2⅛″ × the fabric width.

* Cut these in matching sets of one 20″-long strip and two 10″-long strips.

** Cut these in matching sets of two 20″-long strips and one 10″-long strip.

Making the Blocks

(Arrows indicate pressing direction.)

1. Sew one 1½″ × 20″ Fabric A strip between 2 matching 1½″ × 20″ Fabric B strips to make a strip set. Press. Cut the strip set into twelve 1½″ segments.

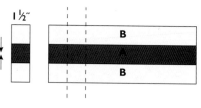

Cut 12 segments.

2. Using the same combination of fabrics that you used in Step 1, sew one 1½″ × 10″ Fabric B strip between two 1½″ × 10″ Fabric A strips. Press. Cut the strip set into six 1½″ segments.

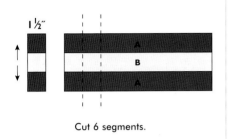

Cut 6 segments.

3. Sew 1 segment from Step 2 between 2 segments from Step 1 to make a Nine-Patch block. Press. Make 6.

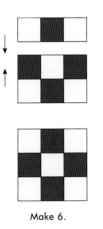

Make 6.

4. Repeat Steps 1–3 to make a total of 102 Nine-Patch blocks in matching groups of 6.

Quilt Assembly

1. Arrange the Nine-Patch blocks and the 3½″ Fabric C squares in 15 horizontal rows of 13 blocks/squares each, alternating them as shown in the assembly diagram. Sew the blocks and squares together into rows. Press the seams toward the Fabric C squares. Sew the rows together. Press.

Assembly diagram

2. Sew a Fabric B triangle right sides together with a Fabric C triangle. Press. Make 56.

Make 56.

3. Sew 15 units from Step 2 together to make a pieced border. Press. Repeat to make a second 15-unit border. Refer to the photo (page 37) and the quilt assembly diagram (page 39), noting the slight variation in the arrangement of the triangles. Press. Sew the appropriate borders to the left and right sides of the quilt. Press the seams toward the borders.

4. Sew 13 units from Step 2 together to make a pieced border as shown in the quilt assembly diagram (page 39) and the photo (page 37). Press. Make 2. Sew a remaining Nine-Patch block to opposite ends of each border. Press. Sew a border to the top and bottom of the quilt. Press the seams toward the border.

Finishing

1. Refer to the diagram below for suggested quilting motifs. The cable patterns appear on the pullout page.

2. Follow the instructions in Preparing the Quilt (pages 13–15) to mark, layer, and baste your quilt.

3. Machine quilt as desired.

4. Sew the 2⅛″-wide Fabric D strips together end to end with diagonal seams and press the seams open. Use this to bind the edges of the quilt; refer to Binding (page 52).

Suggested quilting motifs

'ROUND THE TWIST

Pieced by Alex Anderson, 2004. Machine quilted by Paula Reid.

Finished quilt size: 55½" × 67½"

Finished block size: 6" × 6"

Number of Snowball blocks: 32

Number of Bright Hopes blocks: 31

Skill level: Confident beginner

'Round the Twist has become something of a modern quilt classic. It's easy to cut and piece, and the alternating Snowball and Bright Hopes blocks create a wonderful overall pattern.

You can take this simple design to a new level with some nifty machine quilting. Paula Reid quilted this quilt the way I love best: very classic and traditional. The Bright Hopes blocks are quilted with a walking foot in a crosshatched grid. The easy curves of a free-motion floral motif grace the center of each Snowball block, softening the geometry of the piecework. The quilting is finished with a traditional fan pattern in the border—great for mastering gentle curves.

Materials

Fabric amounts are based on a 42" fabric width.

Assorted pink prints: 1½ yards *total* for blocks and binding (**Fabric A**)

Assorted green prints: 1 yard *total* for blocks (**Fabric B**)

Tone-on-tone cream print: 1⅝ yards for blocks (**Fabric C**)

Coordinating stripe: ¼ yard for inner border (**Fabric D**)

Coordinating floral print: 1⅔ yards for outer border (**Fabric E**)

Backing: 3½ yards

Batting: 60" × 72"

Cutting

All measurements include ¼" seam allowances.

From the assorted pink prints (Fabric A)

Cut a *total* of 64 squares 2" × 2".

Cut a *total* of 62 pieces 2" × 5".

Cut a *total* of 7 strips 2⅛" × the fabric width.

From the assorted green prints (Fabric B)

Cut a *total* of 64 squares 2" × 2".

Cut a *total* of 62 pieces 2" × 5".

From the tone-on-tone cream print (Fabric C)

Cut 6 strips 6½" × the fabric width; crosscut into 32 squares 6½" × 6½".

Cut 3 strips 3½" × the fabric width; crosscut into 31 squares 3½" × 3½".

From the coordinating stripe (Fabric D)

Cut 5 strips 1" × the fabric width.

From the *lengthwise grain* of the coordinating floral print (Fabric E)

Cut 4 strips 6½" × 55½".

Making the Snowball Blocks

(Arrows indicate pressing direction.)

1. Draw a line diagonally, corner to corner, on the wrong side of each 2" Fabric A and 2" Fabric B square.

2. Place a marked Fabric A square on 2 opposite corners of a 6½" Fabric C square and a marked Fabric B square on each of the remaining 2 corners. Sew directly on the drawn lines and trim the seam allowances to ¼". Press. Make 32.

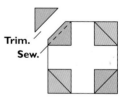

Make 32.

Making the Bright Hopes Blocks

1. With right sides together, align the top edge of a 2″ × 5″ Fabric B piece with the top edge of a 3½″ Fabric C square. Sew the strip to the square. Stop stitching 1″ from the bottom edge of the square. Press.

2. Sew a 2″ × 5″ Fabric A strip, another 2″ × 5″ Fabric B piece, and another 2″ × 5″ Fabric A piece to each remaining side of the unit from Step 1 in the order shown. Press.

3. Complete the seam between B1 and A4. Press.

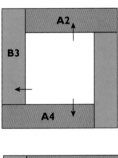

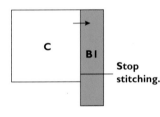

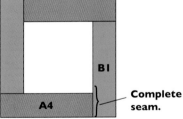

4. Repeat Steps 1–3 to make a total of 31 blocks.

Quilt Assembly

1. Arrange the Snowball blocks and the Bright Hopes blocks in 9 horizontal rows of 7 blocks each, alternating them as shown in the assembly diagram below. Sew the blocks together into rows. Press the seams toward the Bright Hopes blocks. Sew the rows together. Press.

Assembly diagram

2. Refer to Borders (page 51). Sew the 1″-wide Fabric D strips together end to end. Press. Measure the quilt top through the center from top to bottom and cut two 1″-wide strips to this measurement. Sew the trimmed border strips to opposite sides of the quilt. Press the seams toward the border strips.

3. Measure the quilt top through the center from side to side, including the borders you just added. Cut two 1″-wide strips to this measurement. Sew the trimmed border strips to the top and bottom of the quilt. Press the seams toward the border strips.

4. Sew 6½″ × 55½″ Fabric E strips to opposite sides of the quilt. Press the seams toward the outer border. Sew the remaining floral print strips to the top and bottom of the quilt. Press the seams toward the outer border.

Finishing

1. Refer to the diagram below for suggested quilting motifs. The floral motif and fan border patterns appear on the pullout page.

2. Follow the instructions in Preparing the Quilt (pages 13–15) to mark, layer, and baste your quilt.

3. Machine quilt as desired.

4. Sew the assorted 2⅛″-wide Fabric A strips together end to end with diagonal seams and press the seams open. Use this to bind the edges of the quilt; refer to Binding (page 52).

Suggested quilting motifs

Straight Furrows. Pieced and machine quilted by Alex Anderson, 2006.

Finished quilt size: 53″ × 60½″

Finished block size: 7½″ × 7½″

Number of blocks: 56

Skill level: Confident beginner

Here's another favorite design—a variation of the versatile Log Cabin—that I started at a retreat with my quilting buddies. The documentary prints, traditional setting, and lack of borders lend a true nineteenth-century flavor. I inserted a narrow pink piping (also called a thread-catcher) before the binding for a bit of visual pop.

This is an excellent quilt to practice free-motion straight-line quilting. Outfit your machine with the darning foot, drop those feed dogs, and off you go! I quilted each block in the ditch around the diamond and the center square, and down the center of each log, ring by ring. Some of my straight lines are a bit wobbly, but the fabric hides a lot!

Materials

Fabric amounts are based on a 42″ fabric width.

Assorted brown documentary prints: ⅓ yard *total* for blocks (**Fabric A**)

Assorted pink documentary prints: ¼ yard *total* for blocks (**Fabric B**)

Assorted light documentary prints: 2 yards *total* for blocks (**Fabric C**)

Assorted medium and dark documentary prints: 2¼ yards *total* for blocks (**Fabric D**)

Bubble-gum pink documentary print: ¼ yard for piping (**Fabric E**)

Dark brown documentary print: ½ yard for binding (**Fabric F**)

Backing: 3⅓ yards

Batting: 57″ × 65″

Cutting

All measurements include ¼″ seam allowances.

From the assorted brown documentary prints (Fabric A)

Cut a *total* of 224 squares 1¼″ × 1¼″ in matching sets of 4.

From the assorted pink documentary prints (Fabric B)

Cut a *total* of 56 squares 2″ × 2″.

From the assorted light documentary prints (Fabric C)

Cut a *total* of 52 strips 1¼″ × the fabric width.

From the assorted medium and dark documentary prints (Fabric D)

Cut a *total of* 61 strips 1¼″ × the fabric width.

From the bubble-gum pink documentary print (Fabric E)

Cut 6 strips 1″ × the fabric width.

From the dark brown documentary print (Fabric F)

Cut 6 strips 2⅛″ × the fabric width.

Making the Blocks

(Arrows indicate pressing direction.)

1. Draw a line diagonally, corner to corner, on the wrong sides of 4 matching 1¼″ Fabric A squares.

2. Place 1¼″ Fabric A squares on opposite corners of a 2″ Fabric B square, right sides together.

3. Sew directly on the drawn lines and trim the seam allowances to ¼″. Press.

4. Repeat Steps 2 and 3 to sew 1¼″ Fabric A squares to the remaining corners of the unit from Step 3. Trim the seam allowances and press.

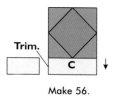

5. Repeat Steps 1–4 to make a total of 56 units.

6. Sew a 1¼″-wide Fabric C strip to each unit from Step 5. Trim the strip even with the raw edge of the unit. Press. Make 56.

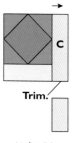

Make 56.

7. Sew a different 1¼″-wide Fabric C strip to an adjacent side of each unit from Step 6. Trim the strip even with the raw edge of the unit. Press. Make 56.

Make 56.

8. Repeat Steps 6 and 7 to sew assorted 1¼″-wide Fabric D strips to the remaining 2 sides of each unit from Step 7. Make 56.

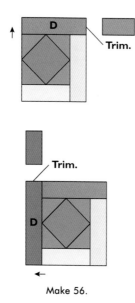

Trim.

Trim.

Make 56.

9. Repeat Steps 6–8 to sew 2 more Fabric C and 2 more Fabric D strips to each unit from Step 8. Make 56.

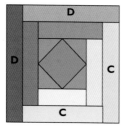

Make 56.

10. Repeat Steps 6–8 to sew 2 more Fabric C and 2 more Fabric D strips each to each unit from Step 9. Make 56.

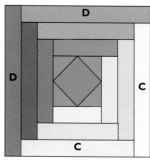

Make 56.

11. Repeat Steps 6–8 to sew a final 2 Fabric C and a final 2 Fabric D strips to each unit from Step 10. Make 56.

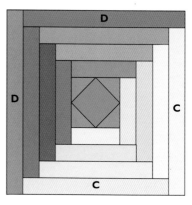

Make 56.

Quilt Assembly

Arrange the blocks in 8 horizontal rows of 7 blocks each as shown in the assembly diagram. Sew the blocks together into rows. Press. Sew the rows together. Press.

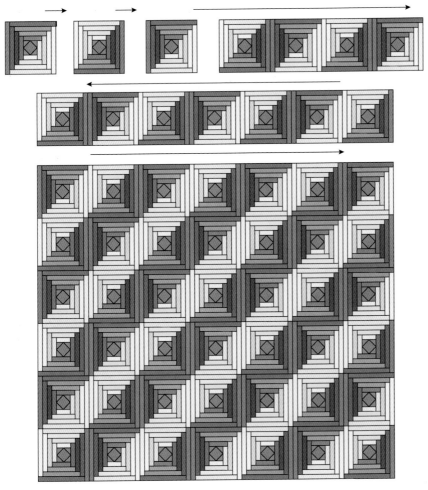

Assembly diagram

Finishing

1. Refer to the diagram below for a suggested quilting motif.

2. Follow the instructions in Preparing the Quilt (pages 13–15) to mark, layer, and baste your quilt.

3. Machine quilt as desired.

4. Sew the 1″-wide Fabric E strips together end to end with diagonal seams and press the seams open. Fold the strip in half, wrong sides together, and press.

5. Trim the batting and backing even with the raw edges of the quilt top. Measure the quilt through the center from top to bottom and from side to side.

Cut 2 strips to each measurement from the long bubble-gum pink piping strip. With right sides together and raw edges aligned, use a machine basting stitch and scant ¼″ seam to sew the piping strips to the sides, top, and bottom of the quilt.

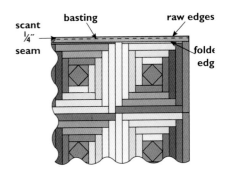

6. Sew the 2⅛″-wide Fabric F strips together end to end with diagonal seams and press the seams open. Use this to bind the edges of the quilt; refer to Binding (page 52).

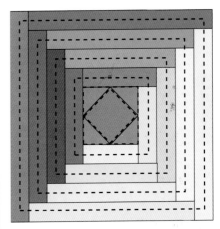

Suggested quilting motif for each block

BASKET IN BLUE

Made and machine quilted by Alex Anderson, 2006.

Finished quilt size: 21″ × 21″

Skill level: Intermediate

In this one, it's all about the quilting! Much like the lovingly hand-stitched quilts of times past, this little whole-cloth piece incorporates all the machine quilting techniques you've mastered. Quilt it in matching thread for a soft, subtle effect or really strut your stuff by quilting in a thread of contrasting color.

Materials

Fabric amounts are based on a 42″ fabric width.

Blue solid: 1⅝ yards for top, backing, and binding (**Fabric A**)

Batting: 25″ × 25″

Cutting

All measurements include ¼″ seam allowances.

From the blue solid (Fabric A)

Cut 1 square 21″ × 21″.

Cut 1 square 25″ × 25″ for backing.

Cut 3 strips 2⅛″ × the fabric width for binding.

Assembling and Finishing

1. Fold the 21″ square of Fabric A in half vertically and horizontally. Press. Unfold and refold diagonally in both directions. Press and unfold the square. The creases you just made are your guidelines for centering the quilt motifs. Refer to the diagram below and use the patterns on the pullout page to mark the creased fabric square.

2. Follow the instructions in Preparing the Quilt (pages 13–15) to mark, layer, and baste your quilt.

3. Machine quilt.

4. Sew the 2⅛″-wide Fabric A strips together end to end with diagonal seams and press the seams open. Use this to bind the edges of the quilt; refer to Binding (page 52).

Suggested quilting motifs

General Instructions

Choosing and Preparing Fabrics

I recommend that you stick with good-quality, 100% cotton fabric. It looks great in the finished quilt, handles well, and holds up nicely over time. I also suggest that you prewash all the fabrics. Cotton can shrink the first time it is washed, so prewashing eliminates the potential for puckers and distortion in the finished quilt. Prewashing can also remove any excess dyes that might bleed or run when the quilt is washed later. Finally, prewashing removes any chemical residue that might linger from the manufacturing process.

Rotary Cutting

I love rotary cutting. It's great for cutting strips and then subcutting them into squares, rectangles, and half- and quarter-square triangles. It's also great for cutting long strips for sashing and borders. If you've never used a rotary cutter before, you might want to read *Rotary Cutting with Alex Anderson* (Recommended Reading, page 54). If the process is new to you, practice on some scrap fabric before starting on your project.

Pinning

Some quilters pin when they piece and some quilters don't. I am a firm believer in pinning because I have found that the little time it takes to pin can determine the success of the block—and, ultimately, the quilt! Basically, I pin wherever there are seams and intersections that need to line up.

I strongly recommend that you invest in a package or two of quality pins. My favorites are extra-fine (1⅜″/0.50mm) glass-head pins. They are a bit more expensive than regular pins, but believe me, they are worth the investment.

Piecing

Set the stitch length on your sewing machine just long enough so that your seam ripper will slide nicely under the stitches. Backtacking is not necessary if the seam ends will be crossed by other seams. Use a ¼″ seam allowance unless instructed otherwise.

Pressing

I usually press seams to one side or the other, but in some cases—for example, if six or more seams are converging in one area—I press the seams open to reduce the bulk. I've included arrows on the illustrations to indicate which way to press the seams.

Settings

Setting (or set) refers to the way the blocks are arranged and sewn before the borders are added. With the exception of *Floral Fiesta* (page 31), which is a medallion-style quilt, and *Basket in Blue* (page 48), which involves no piecing, all the quilts in this book feature some variation of the straight setting. The blocks are placed in rows with the sides parallel to the quilt edges. Once you are satisfied with how the blocks are arranged, sew them into vertical or horizontal rows and press them as instructed in the project directions. After the rows have been sewn, sew each row to the next until the top is complete.

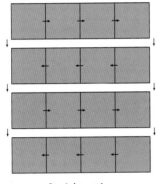

Straight setting

Borders

The quilts in this book feature two different border treatments: butted borders and borders with corner squares.

Butted Borders

Butted borders are the easiest of all borders to stitch, and I have used them for the majority of quilts you see in these pages. All the joining seams are straight, with the borders forming a T where they meet at the corners.

1. Measure the sewn and pressed quilt top through the center from top to bottom. Trim 2 borders to this measurement, piecing them first, if necessary, to achieve the required length. These will be the side borders.

2. Find and mark the midpoint of the side of the quilt top and the midpoint of a side border strip by folding each in half. With right sides together, pin the border to the quilt top, matching ends and midpoint, and pinning every 2˝ in between, easing or stretching slightly to fit. Sew the border to the quilt top with a ¼˝ seam and press as shown. Repeat for the other side border.

3. Measure the quilt from side to side, including the borders you just added. Cut 2 borders to this measurement, piecing them if necessary. These will be the top and bottom borders.

4. Repeat Step 2 to pin and sew the borders to the top and bottom of the quilt. Press as shown.

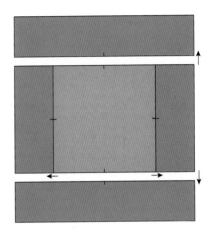

Borders with Corner Squares

Borders with corner squares are easy to sew and—here's a little bonus—can come to your rescue if you run short of border fabric.

1. Measure your quilt top through the center from top to bottom as described in Butted Borders, Step 1. Cut two borders to this measurement, piecing them if necessary to achieve the required length.

2. Repeat Step 1, this time measuring your quilt from side to side for the top and bottom borders.

3. Stitch the side borders to the quilt as described in Butted Borders, Step 2.

4. Stitch corner squares onto both ends of the top and bottom borders and press as shown.

5. Stitch the borders from Step 4 to the top and bottom of the quilt, carefully matching the corner seams to the side borders. Press.

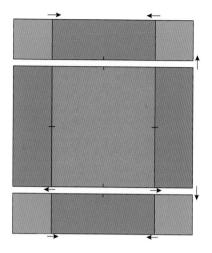

Binding

1. Trim the batting and backing even with the raw edges of the quilt top.

2. Cut 2⅛″-wide strips from the fabric width, as directed in the project instructions. Sew the strips together end to end with diagonal seams and press the seams open. This helps prevent a big lump in the binding.

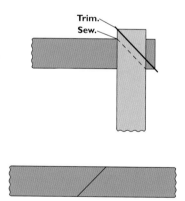

3. Fold the binding in half lengthwise, wrong sides together, and press.

4. With raw edges even, pin the binding to the edge of the quilt, starting a few inches from a corner, leaving the first few inches of the binding unattached. Start sewing, using a ¼″ seam allowance. For pucker-free bindings, use a walking foot.

5. Stop ¼″ from the first corner and backstitch 1 stitch. Adjust the needle position to achieve the desired seam allowance for the next side.

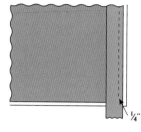

Stitch to ¼″ from corner.

6. Raise the presser foot and lift the needle out of the fabric. Rotate the quilt a quarter turn. Fold the binding at a right angle so that it extends straight above the quilt.

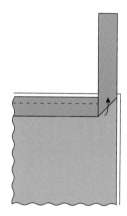

7. Fold the binding strip down so that the raw edge is again even with the edge of the quilt. Begin sewing at the folded edge. Stop ¼″ from the next corner and backstitch 1 stitch.

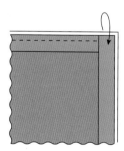

8. Repeat in the same manner at all corners. Stop sewing several inches from where you started stitching the binding to the quilt.

9. Fold the ending binding tail back on itself where it meets the beginning binding tail. From the fold, measure and mark the cut width (2⅛″) of your binding strip. Cut the ending binding tail to this measurement. This will allow enough overlap of the beginning and ending binding tails to join the ends of the binding with a diagonal seam.

10. Open both tails. Place one tail on top of the other at right angles, right sides together. Mark a diagonal line and stitch on the line. Trim the seam to ¼″. Press the seam open. Refold the binding strip and finish stitching it to the quilt.

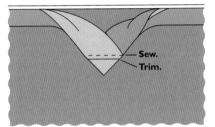

11. Turn the folded edge of the binding over the raw edge of the quilt and slipstitch the binding to the backing. Form miters at the corners.

Quilt Labels

I always encourage quiltmakers to label their quilts. The information you include will be treasured for generations to come. Use a permanent fabric pen on the back (or even on the front) of the quilt or use a beautiful patch, designed specifically for the quilt with embroidery or colorful fabric pens. Before sewing the label to the quilt, consider also writing the same information directly on the quilt (in the area that will be covered by the label) to ensure that the information will not be lost if the label is removed.

RECOMMENDED READING

Anderson, Alex, *Beautifully Quilted with Alex Anderson*, C&T Publishing: Lafayette, CA, 2003

_____, *Hand Quilting with Alex Anderson*, C&T Publishing: Lafayette, CA, 1998

_____, *Rotary Cutting with Alex Anderson*, C&T Publishing: Lafayette, CA, 1999

Gaudynski, Diane, *Guide to Machine Quilting*, American Quilter's Society: Paducah, KY, 2002

_____, *Quilt Savvy: Gaudynski's Machine Quilting Guidebook*, American Quilter's Society: Paducah, KY, 2006

Hargrave, Harriet, *Heirloom Machine Quilting*, 4th Ed., C&T Publishing: Lafayette, CA, 2004

Nickels, Sue, *Machine Quilting: A Primer of Techniques*, American Quilter's Society: Paducah, KY, 2003

Soltys, Karen Costello (editor), *Fast & Fun Machine Quilting*, Rodale Press: Emmaus, PA, 1997

RESOURCES

Bernina of America
3702 Prairie Lake Court
Aurora, IL 60504
Phone: (630) 978-2500
Fax: (630) 978-8214
questions@berninausa.com
www.berninausa.com/home.jsp

Superior Threads
P.O. Box 1672
St. George, UT 84771
Phone: (800) 499-1777
Fax: (435) 628-6385
info@superiorthreads.com
www.superiorthreads.com

Ferd. Schmetz Needle Corp.
9960 NW 116 Way, Suite 3
Medley, FL 33178
Phone: (305) 889-2080
Fax: (305) 889-2082
schmetz@bellsouth.net
www.schmetz.com

Batts in the Attic
3114 Tournament Drive
Palmdale, CA 93551
Fluff & Stuff: Machine Quilting with Paula Reid (DVD)
info@battsintheattic.com
www.battsintheattic.com

ABOUT THE AUTHOR

Alex Anderson's love affair with quiltmaking began in 1978, when she completed her *Grandmother's Flower Garden* quilt as part of her work toward a degree in art at San Francisco State University. Over the years, her focus has rested on understanding fabric relationships and on an intense appreciation for traditional quilting surface design and star quilts.

For eleven years, Alex hosted television's premier quilt show, *Simply Quilts*, and is spokesperson for Bernina of America. Her quilts have appeared in numerous magazines, often in articles devoted specifically to her work.

Alex has two children and lives in Northern California with her husband, their cat, and the challenges of feeding various forms of wildlife in her backyard. Visit her website at http://alexandersonquilts.com.

Other Books by Alex Anderson

Great Titles
from C&T PUBLISHING

Available at your local retailer or
www.ctpub.com or 800.284.1114